Copyright 2021

All right reserved. No part of this book should be reproduced without express permission of the author.

Reproduction of all or any part of this book is punishable under relevant law.

Table of Contents

PREVIEW 4
PANCREATITIS DIET RECIPES 5
BREAKFAST 5
   1. Steel Cut Oats – Stick To Your Ribs! 5
   2. Walnut Pumpkin Pancakes 7
   3. Waldorf Salad 9
   4. Chicken Salad Blues 11
   5. Orange-Walnut Salad 12
   6. Warm Eggplant and Goat Cheese Sandwiches 13
   7. Tomato Crostini 15
   8. Blood Orange and Duck Confit Salad 17
   9. Rosemary-Roasted New Potatoes 19
   10. Southeastern Seasoned Catfish 21
LUNCH 22
   11. Creamy Soup 22
   12. Chicken Taco Salad 24
   13. Slow Cooker Cream Cheese Chicken Chili 26
   14. Shrimp Spring Rolls 28
   15. Kale Mushroom Salad 30
   16. Tuna Stuffed Potatoes 32
   17. Homemade Granola 34
   18. Light Meal Made Of Lemon-Garlic Shrimp and Vegetables 37
   19. Chicken And Rice With A Pinch Thyme 39
   20. Steak Salad 42

DINNERS 44

21. Stuffed Capsicum 44

22. Cooker Beef Stew 46

23. Cheesy Baked Pasta With Mushrooms 49

24. Moussaka 51

25. Chicken Hot Pot Pie 53

26. Mushroom risotto 55

27. Delicious Food 57

28. Rice and Chicken 59

29. Delicious & Nutritious Crispy Salmon 61

30. Bread and Butter pudding 63

SNACKS 65

31. Lemon and Blueberry Muffin 65

32. Lemon cookie 67

33. Vegetarian sausage rolls 69

34. Pancake Mix 71

35. Gluten Free Chocolate Chip Cookies 73

36. Healthy Carrot cake 75

37. Awesome Blueberry Pancakes 77

38. Zucchini slice 79

39. Apple Pie 81

40. Roasted Pumpkin Pikelets 84

PREVIEW

Pancreatitis occurs when digestive enzymes become activated while still in the pancreas, irritating the cells of your pancreas and causing inflammation. With repeated bouts of acute pancreatitis, damage to the pancreas can occur and lead to chronic pancreatitis.

PANCREATITIS DIET RECIPES

BREAKFAST

1. Steel Cut Oats – Stick To Your Ribs!

Ingredients

- Three cups good, clean filtered water
- One cup of organically grown high-quality steel cut oats
- Quarter cup frozen organic blueberries
- Half a banana
- Quarter cup of walnuts
- Whole, raw milk
- Organic butter from grass-fed cows
- Maple syrup
- Cinnamon
- Full spectrum sea salt

Instructions

1. Bring 3 cups good, clean filtered water to a boil, then add one cup of organically grown, high-quality steel cut oats and a pinch of full spectrum sea salt. When the water returns to a boil, reduce the heat to a

simmer for about 30 minutes. Cover with a lid but keep it cracked and stir occasionally.
2. When close to finished, add blueberries, banana in slices, walnuts and a pat of butter. Stir until everything is mixed well and completely hot.
3. Then put a few scoops in a bowl, add milk, (whole raw milk) to make it creamy, a pinch of cinnamon, and a SMALL splash of real maple syrup.
4. Steel cut oats are very different from cheap, instant types of rolled oats. The oat kernels are chopped and the germ is left intact. As Dr. Weil says, they digest much more slowly, delivering their nutrient value more efficiently – which is why steel cut oats are one of the very clean gout diet recipes.
5. I like to eat steel cut oats with a slice of high-quality, organically grown Canadian Bacon.

2. Walnut Pumpkin Pancakes

Ingredients

- Half cup of organic canned pumpkin
- Half cup of organic plain yogurt
- Half cup of chopped walnuts
- One banana
- ¼ teaspoon of aluminum free baking soda
- One organic, free-range large egg yolk
- Quarter cup of organic whole wheat (or spelt) flour
- Four organic, free-range large egg whites
- Quarter teaspoon sea salt
- Quarter teaspoon of cayenne
- Organic butter from grass-fed cows
- Real maple syrup

Instructions

1. In a big bowl, whisk the pumpkin, yogurt, walnuts, baking soda, egg yolk, and flour. Then in another bowl, whisk the egg whites, sea salt and cayenne together, then fold it into the yogurt and pumpkin mixture.

2. Heat a large cast-iron skillet to medium and melt a generous amount of butter in it. Spoon about a third of a cup of batter on to the skillet for each pancake. When each pancake is full of bubbles and crisp around the edges, turn over and brown the other side.
3. When finished and hot on the plate, melt a generous amount of butter (organic, from grass-fed cows) over each pancake, then put slices of banana on top and use real maple syrup sparingly.
4. For a healthy variation, use freshly ground peanut or almond butter instead of the butter when the pancakes are hot on the plate.
5. Cayenne is a good spice of helping to curb inflammation. Bananas are helpful in alkalizing. Nuts and nut butters provide protein. For extra protein, add a slice of high-quality, organically grown Canadian Bacon.

3. Waldorf Salad

Prep: 10 mins

Total: 10 mins

Makes 4 servings (serving size: 1/2 cup salad and 2 boston or bibb lettuce leaves)

Ingredients

- 2 tablespoons low-fat mayonnaise
- 1 tablespoon lemon juice
- 2 small (Gala or Fuji) apples, cubed
- 1 cup seedless red grapes, halved
- 1/3 cup dried cranberries
- 1/4 cup coarsely chopped walnuts
- 1/4 cup thinly sliced celery (about 1 stalk)
- 8 Boston or Bibb lettuce leaves

Instructions

1. Combine mayonnaise and lemon juice in a medium bowl. Add apples, grapes, and cranberries; mix well.

2. Add the walnuts and celery, and mix well. Serve it on a bed of 2 lettuce leaves. The salad can be refrigerated up to 2 hours before serving.

4. Chicken Salad Blues

Serves: 4

Ingredients

- 1 9.75-ounce can premium chunk chicken breast packed in water
- 1 large stalk celery, finely chopped
- 1/4 cup reduced-fat mayonnaise
- 4 leaves romaine or red leaf lettuce, washed and trimmed
- 2 ounces blue cheese, crumbled
- 1 ripe tomato, quartered (or 8 cherry tomatoes)
- 1 small cucumber, washed and thinly sliced

Instructions

1. Drain chicken. Add chopped celery and mayonnaise. Mix lightly to keep the chicken chunky. Arrange lettuce in a shallow serving bowl. Put chicken salad in the middle and crumble blue cheese over it. Arrange tomatoes and cucumber slices around the plate. Cover with plastic wrap and refrigerate until ready to serve.

5. Orange-Walnut Salad

Serves: 4

Ingredients

- 2 cups romaine lettuce, coarsely chopped (about 6 leaves)
- 1 cup arugula
- 1 cucumber, peeled, quartered lengthwise, seeds removed, and chopped
- 1/4 cup red onion, thinly sliced
- 2 navel oranges, peeled and chopped
- 2 tablespoons walnuts, chopped
- 1 tablespoon walnut oil
- 1 tablespoon red wine vinegar
- 2 ounces blue cheese (gluten-free)

Instructions

1. Layer ingredients in a large salad bowl. Just before serving, sprinkle with walnut oil and vinegar and toss. Crumble blue cheese on top.

6. Warm Eggplant and Goat Cheese Sandwiches

Yield: 2 servings

Ingredients

- 1 teaspoon olive oil
- 2 (1/4-inch) vertical slices small eggplant
- Cooking spray
- 1/4 teaspoon salt
- 1/4 teaspoon freshly ground black pepper
- 1/4 cup (2 ounces) goat cheese, softened
- 2 (1 1/2-ounce) rustic sandwich rolls
- 2 (1/4-inch) slices tomato
- 1 cup arugula

Instructions

1. Preheat oven to 275°.
2. Brush oil over eggplant.
3. Heat a large nonstick skillet coated with cooking spray over medium-high heat. Add eggplant; cook 5 minutes on each side or until lightly browned. Sprinkle with salt and pepper.

4. Spread about 1 tablespoon of goat cheese over cut side of each roll half. Place rolls on a baking sheet, cheese sides up; bake at 275° for 8 to 10 minutes or until thoroughly heated.
5. Remove from oven; top bottom half of each roll with 1 eggplant slice, 1 tomato slice, and 1/2 cup arugula. Top sandwiches with top halves of rolls.

7. Tomato Crostini

Yield:

2 servings (serving size: 2 bread slices and about 1/3 cup tomato mixture)

Ingredients

- 1/2 cup chopped plum tomato
- 1 tablespoon chopped fresh basil
- 1 tablespoon chopped pitted green olives
- 1 teaspoon capers
- 1/2 teaspoon balsamic vinegar
- 1/2 teaspoon olive oil
- 1/8 teaspoon sea salt
- Dash of freshly ground black pepper
- 1 garlic clove, minced
- 4 (1-inch-thick) slices French bread baguette
- Cooking spray
- 1 garlic clove, halved

Instructions

1. Preheat oven to 375º.
2. Combine first 9 ingredients.
3. Lightly coat both sides of bread slices with cooking spray; arrange bread slices in a single layer on a baking sheet. Bake at 375º for 4 minutes on each side or until lightly toasted.
4. Rub 1 side of bread slices with halved garlic; top evenly with tomato mixture.

8. Blood Orange and Duck Confit Salad

Prep Time: 5 mins
Cook Time: 5
Total: 10 mins
Yield: Makes 4 servings (serving size: 1 1/2 cups salad and about 1 1/4 tablespoons dressing)

Ingredients

- 1 tablespoon sherry vinegar
- 4 blood oranges, divided (3 sectioned, about 1 cup; 1 juiced, about 1/4 cup)
- 1 teaspoon Dijon mustard
- 1 tablespoon olive oil
- 1/4 teaspoon salt
- 1/4 teaspoon pepper
- 1 small duck confit leg (5-6 ounces), shredded, skin, fat, and bones discarded (about 3/4 cup)
- 6 cups mixed winter salad greens (such as romaine, escarole, and spinach)
- 1/4 cup skinned chopped hazelnuts, toasted

Instructions

1. In a small bowl, combine vinegar, orange juice, mustard, and oil, whisking well. Whisk in salt and pepper.
2. In a large bowl, combine shredded duck, salad greens, hazelnuts, and orange sections. Drizzle with vinaigrette; serve.

9. Rosemary-Roasted New Potatoes

Prep: 5 mins

Cook: 22 mins

Total: 27 mins

Yield:

Makes 4 servings (serving size: about 3/4 cup)

Ingredients

- 1 (1-pound, 4-ounce) package refrigerated red potato wedges (such as Simply Potatoes)
- 2 tablespoons chopped fresh rosemary
- 3 garlic cloves, crushed
- 1 tablespoon olive oil
- 1/2 teaspoon onion powder
- 1/4 teaspoon salt
- 1/4 teaspoon pepper
- 1/4 teaspoon pepper

Instructions

1. Preheat oven to 500°.

2. In a large bowl, combine potatoes and remaining ingredients.
3. Toss thoroughly to coat each potato wedge with oil and seasonings.
4. Place the potato wedges on a baking sheet that's lined with foil.
5. Bake 22 minutes or until tender and golden. Serve hot.

10. Southeastern Seasoned Catfish

Serves: 2

Ingredients

- 2 boneless, skinless catfish fillets (about 3/4 pound)
- 2 teaspoons dried minced onion
- 1/2 teaspoon paprika
- 1/2 teaspoon garlic powder
- 1/4 teaspoon cayenne pepper
- 1/4 teaspoon mustard powder

Instructions

1. On a sheet of waxed paper, combine dry ingredients. Rinse catfish fillets and pat dry with a paper towel. Coat both sides with rub. Heat broiler to high. Pour about a teaspoon of olive oil on a small cookie sheet and place catfish fillets on it. Broil about 4 inches from heat for about 5 minutes. Turn fillets and broil 3 to 4 minutes longer, until fish is opaque and flakes easily with a fork.

LUNCH

11. Creamy Soup

Servings:12

Ingredients

- 2 quarts water for boiling potatoes
- 8 potatoes diced
- 4 cans chicken broth
- 1 small onion diced
- 1 teaspoon salt
- 1 teaspoon fresh coarse ground black pepper
- 3/4 cup all-purpose flour
- 2 cups cold water
- 1 1/2 cups heavy cream
- 1 cup butter
- 1 1/2 cups colby-monterey jack cheese
- 1/4 cup bacon bit
- 1/4 green onion

Instructions

1. Boil the potatoes for about 8-10 minutes or until tender.

2. In a large pot, add the broth, onions, salt, pepper, and water. Let is simmer on medium low.
3. In a small saucepan, melt the 2 sticks of butter. Whisk in the 3/4 cup flour and add to your broth mixture slowly.
4. Add the heavy cream slowly to thicken.
5. Let that simmer for 20 minutes and add the potatoes.
6. Serve with green onions, bacon, and cheese if you'd like!

12. Chicken Taco Salad

Prep Time: 20 Minutes

Cook Time: 15 Minutes

Total Time: 35 Minutes

Servings: 6

Ingredients

Dressing Ingredients:
- 3/4 cups Ranch Dressing
- 1/4 cup Salsa
- 3 Tablespoons Cilantro finely minced
- Salad Ingredients:
- 2 Chicken Breasts boneless skinless
- 2 Tablespoons taco seasoning
- 2 Tablespoons vegetable oil
- 1 head Green Leaf Lettuce of lettuce of choice shredded
- 3 Roma Tomatoes Diced
- 1/2 cup Grated Pepper Jack Cheese or cheese of choice
- 1/2 cup whole kernel corn
- 2 avocados Diced

- 3 green onions Sliced
- 1/2 cup Cilantro Leaves
- Tortilla Chips crushed

Instructions

1. Prepare the dressing by whisking together the ranch, salsa and cilantro. Set aside.
2. To prepare the chicken, heat the oil on medium high heat. Season each side of the chicken breasts generously with the taco seasoning. Cook the chicken breasts on each side about 4 minutes or until no longer pink. Remove and set aside and cut into cubes.
3. Place the corn into the skillet and cook for a few minutes and remove from heat and set aside.
4. To assemble the salad pile the green leaf lettuce on the bottom. Then pile the chicken, tomatoes, avocado, cheese, green onions, corn, green onions, cilantro leaves and crushed tortillas on top. Drizzle the dressing on the top and serve.

13. Slow Cooker Cream Cheese Chicken Chili

Prep Time: 10 Minutes

Cook Time: 4 Hours

Total Time: 4 Hours 10 Minutes

Servings: 10

Ingredients

- 2 chicken breasts can use fresh or frozen
- 1 can Rotel Tomatoes
- 1 can corn kernels do not drain
- 1 can black beans rinsed and drained
- 1 package ranch dressing mix
- 1 Tablespoon cumin
- 1 teaspoon chili powder
- 1 teaspoon onion powder
- 1 package (8 oz) fat free cream cheese

Instructions

1. Spray Slow cooker with cooking spray and lay chicken breasts in the bottom.

2. Dump the can of undrained corn, drained and rinsed black beans, and rotel on top of the chicken.
3. Put ranch seasoning packet, chili powder, onion powder and cumin on top.
4. Stir to combine and top with block of cream cheese.
5. Cook on low for 4-6. Stir if you can after about 2-3 hours.

14. Shrimp Spring Rolls

Prep Time: 20 Minutes

Cook Time: 5 Minutes

Total Time: 25 Minutes

Servings: 4 People

Ingredients

- 10 Rice Paper Roll Sheets
- 1 pound medium Shrimps shelled and deveined
- 1 tsp Salt
- 1 head Romaine Lettuce leaves removed and cleaned
- 1 cup julienned Carrots
- 1 cup julienned Cucumber
- 1 cup fresh Mint Leaves

Instructions

1. Bring a pot of water to boil and add a teaspoon of salt to it, along with shrimp. Boil for 2-3 minutes and drain the shrimp. Once cool, slice each shrimp in half lengthwise. Set aside.

2. Fill a shallow round dish with water. Take a rice paper sheet and submerge it completely in the water for 10

seconds. Then remove and place it flat on a chopping board or kitchen towel.

3. Working quickly, place one lettuce leaf towards the bottom of the rice paper. Place a few julienned of cucumber, carrots and a few mint leaves on the lettuce.

4. Now wrap the bottom edge of the rice paper over the filling (refer to the pictures above), and then place both sides over it (like a burrito). Roll it up once more and then place three pieces of sliced shrimp in the middle side by side. Continue rolling the rice paper over the shrimp till its tightly rolled.

5. Repeat till all the rice paper and filling is used up. Serve fresh with a dipping sauce on the side.

15. Kale Mushroom Salad

Prep Time: 25 mins

Servings : 4

Ingredients

- 6 cups of thinly sliced kale, stems removed
- 2 slices of center-cut bacon
- 2 coarsely chopped hard-boiled eggs
- ½ cup chopped onions
- 2 teaspoons whole-grain mustard
- 2 tablespoons of extra-virgin olive oil
- 2 tablespoons of red-wine vinegar
- ¼ teaspoon of freshly ground pepper
- Pinch of salt

Instructions

1. Start by massaging the kale with a bit of sea salt, olive oil, and lemon juice. Let it sit like that while you prepare the rest of the veggies. It will be much tastier if you use kale this way instead of plain and raw.
2. Take a large bowl and place kale and eggs in it.
3. Turn on your stove on medium heat and use a large skillet to cook bacon, until it becomes crispy. Leave

the bacon fat in the skillet. Transfer the bacon to a plate lined with towel paper. Once the bacon is cool enough, chop it into bite-sized pieces.

4. Add olive oil and chopped onions to the pan and cook, continuously stirring, for about 2 minutes.

5. Add mushrooms and keep stirring for 2 more minutes, until they are softened. Once the mushrooms are ready, remove the pan from the heat and stir in mustard, vinegar, salt, and pepper.

6. Pour the mushroom mixture over eggs and kale. Add the bacon to the bowl and toss to combine. Bon Appétit!

16. Tuna Stuffed Potatoes

Prep Time: 40

Servings: 4

Ingredients

- 2 drained 5-6-ounce cans of chunk light tuna
- 4 scrubbed medium russet potatoes
- 1 drained and chopped 6-ounce jar of marinated artichoke hearts
- ¾ cup of low-fat Greek yogurt
- ½ cup and 2 tablespoons of fresh basil.
- 1 tablespoon of rinsed capers
- 2 chopped scallions
- 1 finely chopped plum tomato
- ¾ cup of shredded provolone cheese
- ¼ teaspoon of salt
- ½ teaspoon of ground pepper

Instructions

1. Take the potatoes and pierce them all over using a fork. Microwave potatoes on medium heat for about 20 minutes, until they are soft. Remember to turn them once or twice, so they get cooked evenly. If your

microwave offers such option, use the "potato setting."

2. In the meantime, combine tuna with yogurt, basil, scallions, chopped artichoke hearts, capers, salt, and pepper. Use a large bowl to do so.
3. Once potatoes are cool enough to handle, cut off the top third from each one. Use a spoon to scoop out the insides. Mix scooped potato insides with the tuna.
4. Prepare a microwave-safe dish and place the potato shells in it. Use a fork or the potato masher to mash the tuna-potato mixture together.
5. Divide the mixture among the potato shells and top it with cheese. Place the dish back into the microwave and turn on the high heat. Let it cook for 2-4 minutes until the cheese is melted and filling is hot.
6. Top each potato with remaining basil and a little bit of tomato. Your lunch is ready to be served.

17. Homemade Granola

Prep Time: 30

Total Time: N/A

Servings: 16

Ingredients

- 4 cups of rolled oats
- 1 ½ cup of raw nuts and seeds (you can use whichever you like the best, but in this case, we will go with pecans and pepitas)
- ⅔ cup of chopped dried fruit, preferably cherries and bananas
- ½ cup of melted coconut or olive oil
- ½ cup of maple syrup or raw honey
- 1 teaspoon of fine-grain sea salt1
- ½ teaspoon of cinnamon
- 1 teaspoon of vanilla extract
- ½ cup of coconut flakes or chocolate chips

Instructions

1. Preheat your oven to 350° F and use a parchment paper to line a large, rimmed baking sheet.

2. Take a large mixing bowl, throw in the oats, nuts, seeds, cinnamon, and salt. Stir the mixture to blend it together.

3. Add the oil, maple syrup or honey and vanilla extract. Mix ingredients well, until everything seems lightly coated.

4. Pour the granola into the pan. Take a large spoon and spread the granola to form an even layer. Place the pan in the oven and bake for 21-23 minutes until granola turns to gold. Stir halfway. You don't have to worry if it doesn't seem crispy enough once you take it out of the oven, it will further crisp up on its own as it cools.

5. Let it cool completely, before breaking it into pieces. Then stir in the dried fruit and chocolate chips or coconut flakes.

6. You can store the granola in airtight containers at room temperature for up to 2 weeks. If you

choose to store it in sealed freezer bags in the freezer, it can last up to 3 months.

18. Light Meal Made Of Lemon-Garlic Shrimp and Vegetables

Prep Time: 40

Total Time: N/A

Servings: 4

Ingredients

- 1 pound of peeled and deveined raw shrimp
- 1 cup of reduced-sodium chicken broth
- 2 large diced red bell peppers

- 2 tablespoons of lemon juice
- 1 teaspoon of cornstarch
- 4 teaspoons of extra-virgin olive oil
- 5 minced cloves of garlic
- 2 pounds of trimmed asparagu.

- 2 teaspoons of fresh lemon zest

- 2 tablespoons of chopped fresh parsley

- ½ teaspoon of salt

Instructions

1. 1.Take a large nonstick skillet and place it over medium-high heat. Heat two teaspoons of olive oil in it. Add the asparagus, bell peppers, lemon zest and ¼ teaspoon of salt. Cook for 6 minutes, while stirring occasionally.
2. Once vegetables beginning to soften, transfer to a bowl and cover with a lid to keep them warm.
3. Add the rest of the olive oil and garlic to the pan and cook for 30 seconds. Stir, until it turns fragrant.
4. Throw the shrimp in and cook for 1 minute, continuously stirring.
5. 5Mix the chicken broth with cornstarch in a small bowl. Whisk it until it is smooth and add the mixture to the pan. Sprinkle it with the remaining salt. Cook while stirring for 2 more minutes, until the sauce is optimally thick and the shrimp are pink.
6. Remove the pan from the heat. Mix in the parsley and lemon juice. Your lunch is ready to be served.

19. Chicken And Rice With A Pinch Thyme

Prep Time: 1 hour 20 minutes

Servings: 6

Ingredients

- 5 chicken thigh fillets
- 1 chopped onion
- 2 minced garlic cloves
- 1 ½ cups of long grain white rice
- 1 ½ cups of warm chicken broth
- 1 ¼ cups of warm water

For The Chicken Rub

- 1 teaspoon of paprika powder
- 1 teaspoon dried thyme
- ½ teaspoon of garlic powder
- ½ teaspoon of onion powder
- ¾ teaspoon of salt

- Black pepper to taste

Instructions

1. Preheat the oven to 350° F.

2. Prepare a baking dish and scatter onion and garlic around it. Place butter in the center. Bake garlic and onions for 15 minutes, but make sure to check them at 12 minutes and mix them if you notice some bits are browning more than they should.

3. In the meantime, combine together the ingredients for the chicken rub. Sprinkle it on both sides of the meat.

4. Remove the baking dish from the oven and add rice. Mix it all together. Place chicken on top of rice and pour chicken broth and water around it.

5. Cover the baking dish with aluminum foil, and place it back in the oven for additional 35 minutes.

6. Remove the foil and bake for 15 more minutes.

7. Leave it to sit for 5 minutes, then remove the chicken and fluff the rice up. Enjoy your traditional lunch!

20. Steak Salad

Prep Time: 25 minutes

Servings: 4

Ingredients

- 1 zested and juiced lime
- ⅓ cup of olive oil
- 2 minced garlic cloves
- 1 tablespoon of Dijon mustard
- ½ teaspoon of ground cumin
- ½ teaspoon of salt
- ½ teaspoon of freshly grounded black pepper

Instructions

1. Start by preparing the vinaigrette. Take a small bowl or measuring cup. Add all of the ingredients and whisk until they are all thoroughly mixed.

2. Proceed to make a salad. Place the sliced steak on a large platter. Add lettuce, red onion, bell pepper, black beans, queso fresco and corn in a large bowl. Pour several tablespoons of vinaigrette over the salad. Use salad tongs to toss the mixture, until lettuce is lightly coated.

3. Top the steak with dressed salad. Arrange avocado and hardboiled eggs atop of it. At last, sprinkle the salad with cilantro, and you are ready to enjoy your meal.

DINNERS

21. Stuffed Capsicum

Ingredients

- 6 large capsicums (a mixture of colours)
- 1 tablespoon vegetable oil
- 1 small zucchini, finely chopped
- 2 cloves garlic, crushed
- 1 tablespoon freshly squeezed lemon juice
- 2 cups cooked couscous
- 1 can (400 g) chickpeas, drained and rinsed
- 1 medium ripe tomato, seeded and finely chopped
- 1 teaspoon dried oregano
- ½ teaspoon salt
- ¼ teaspoon black pepper
- ½ cup (75 g) crumbled feta cheese

Instructions

1. Slice the tops off the capsicums to make lids. Scoop out seeds and membranes; discard. Simmer the capsicums and lids in a large saucepan of lightly salted

boiling water, covered, for 5 minutes. Drain and set aside.

2. Preheat oven to 180°C. Heat oil in a medium saucepan over medium heat. Add zucchini and garlic and sauté 2 minutes. Stir in juice. Cook 1 minute and remove from heat. Stir in the couscous, chickpeas, tomato, oregano, salt, pepper and feta.

3. Fill each capsicum with couscous mixture. Place upright in a shallow baking dish. Cover with capsicum lids. Bake just until filling is heated through, about 20 minutes

22. Cooker Beef Stew

Ingredients

- 1 kg beef chuck roast, trimmed and cubed
- 3 tablespoons plus 2 teaspoons sea salt
- 4 tablespoons olive oil, divided
- 1 large onion, chopped
- 1 large leek, halved lengthwise, sliced crosswise
- 4 garlic cloves, finely grated
- 1 tablespoon tomato paste
- 1 cup dry white wine
- 1 bay leaf
- 1 cup chicken broth
- 1 teaspoon freshly ground black pepper
- 3 large carrots, peeled and cut into pieces
- 3 celery stalks, sliced
- 1 large parsnip, peeled and cut into pieces
- 5 medium red waxy potatoes, quartered, halved if small
- 8 ounces crimini mushrooms, quartered
- Chopped parsley and chopped chives (for serving)

Instructions

1. Season roast with 3 tbsp of salt, rubbing into the grain and covering all sides. Wrap tightly in plastic and chill for at least 3 hours.

2. Heat 2 tbsp of oil in a medium skillet over high heat and place the onion, leek, and remaining 2 tsp of salt, stirring occasionally, until browned around the edges but not completely cooked through for 6–8 minutes. Add garlic and tomato paste and cook for about 1 minute. Next, add wine and bay leaf and cook, stirring occasionally for about 2 minutes or until alcohol has evaporated. Scrape onion mixture into ceramic then insert into your slow cooker. Stir in broth and pepper.

3. Heat remaining 2 Tbsp. oil in the same skillet over high heat. Cook roast, turning occasionally, until golden brown on all sides for 10–12 minutes. Transfer it to a slow cooker. Arrange carrots, celery, parsnip, potatoes, and mushrooms around roast, pushing into onion mixture and surrounding meat.

4. Cook over high heat until the roast is very tender and shreds easily for 7–8 hours. If you need to program

your slow cooker, set for 7 hours at high, then set to warm after that.

23. Cheesy Baked Pasta With Mushrooms

Ingredients

- 1 large onion, chopped
- 2 sticks celery, thinly sliced
- 1 leek,
- 2 garlic cloves, chopped
- A handful of button mushrooms, sliced
- 1 jar pasta sauce
- 300g whole wheat penne
- Grated cheese, for topping.

Instructions

1. Heat a splash of oil in a frying pan, add the onion, and celery, season with pepper and a little salt, then cook until soft. Add the garlic and cook for a little while longer, until the garlic is soft. Remove vegetables and set aside.

2. Add a splash of oil into another pan and add the mushrooms.

3. Return the cooked veg to the frying pan, add the pasta sauce bring to the boil and simmer for 5-10 minutes.

4. Heat oven to 200C. Cook the pasta according to pack instructions. Drain, stir into the vegetables and spoon into a large lasagne dish.

5. Spoon grated cheese over the top of the pasta and bake for 20-25 mins or until lightly browned.

6. Serve with garlic bread for better enjoyment.

24. Moussaka

Ingredients

Servings 2

Prep time + cook time: 30 minutes

- 1 tbsp extra virgin olive oil
- ½ onion, finely chopped
- 1 garlic clove, finely chopped
- 250g / 9 oz lean beef mince
- 200g can / 1 cup chopped tomatoes
- 1 tbsp tomato purée
- 1 tsp ground cinnamon
- 200g can / 1 cup chickpeas
- 100g pack / ⅔ cup feta cheese, crumbled
- Mint (fresh preferable)
- Brown bread, to serve

Instructions

1. Heat the oil in a pan. Add the onion and garlic and fry until soft. Add the mince and fry for 3-4 minutes until browned.

2. Tip the tomatoes into the pan and stir in the tomato purée and cinnamon, then season. Leave the mince to simmer for 20 minutes. Add the chickpeas halfway through.

3. Sprinkle the feta and mint over the mince. Serve with toasted bread.

25. Chicken Hot Pot Pie

Ingredients

- 2 onions
- 600 g free-range chicken thighs, skin off, bone out
- 350 g mixed mushrooms
- 1 bunch of fresh thyme (30g)
- 375 g block of all-butter puff pastry, (cold)

Instructions

1. Preheat the oven to 220 degrees C. Place a 30cm non-stick ovenproof frying pan on a high heat, with a smaller non-stick pan on a medium heat alongside. Pour 1 tablespoon of olive oil into the larger pan.

2. Peel and roughly chop the onions, adding them to the larger pan as you go. Roughly chop two-thirds of the thighs, finely chop the rest, and add to the onion pan. Cook for 6 minutes, or until golden, stirring occasionally.

3. Meanwhile, place the mushrooms in the dry pan, tearing up any larger ones. Let them toast and get nutty for 4 minutes, then tip into the chicken pan and strip in half the thyme leaves.

4. Remove the pan from the heat, add a pinch of sea salt and black pepper, then stir in 1 tablespoon of red wine vinegar and 150ml of water.

5. Working quickly, roll out the pastry so it's 2cm bigger than the pan, then place it over the filling, using a wooden spoon to push it into the edges.

6. Very lightly criss-cross the pastry, then brush with 1 teaspoon of olive oil. Poke the remaining thyme sprigs into the middle of the pie.

7. Bake at the bottom of the oven for 15 minutes, or until golden and puffed up.

26. Mushroom risotto

Ingredients

- 3 cups mushrooms
- 10 cups chicken stock in hot water
- 1 teaspoon sugar
- 2 tablespoons extra-virgin olive oil
- 1 cup arborio rice
- 1 cup shredded parmesan or romano cheese

Instructions

1.

    Combine the mushrooms, stock, and sugar in a large bowl and allow to stand for 30 minutes. Pour the liquid into a pan through a fine strainer or through cheesecloth to remove any sand or grit, and bring it to a simmer.

    Carefully wash the mushrooms, remove the tough stems, and cut them into thin strips. Set aside. Heat the olive oil in a heavy pan over medium heat. Add the rice and stir until each grain of rice is coated and shiny, about 2 minutes. Spoon 1/2 cup of the hot mushroom liquid into the rice and cook, stirring frequently, until it is almost absorbed. Add the mushrooms and mix well.

Continue to add the liquid, 1/2 cup at a time, stirring constantly between additions until it has all been added, about 20 minutes. Always wait until the previous 1/2 cup has been almost absorbed, but do not wait until the rice is dry before adding more liquid. There should always be a veil of liquid over the top of the rice and the final consistency should be slightly runny, like a soft-textured cooked cereal. Remove from the heat and stir the cheese into the risotto.

27. Delicious Food

Ingredients

- 400g rhubarb
- 1 vanilla pod or ½ teaspoon vanilla paste
- 75g golden caster sugar
- 2 teaspoons cornflour

Crumble

- 100g cold unsalted butter, plus extra for greasing
- 150g plain flour
- 50g golden caster sugar

Instructions

1. Preheat the oven to 200°C. Grease an ovenproof dish with a little butter.

    Chop the rhubarb into 3cm pieces, halving any thicker pieces lengthways. Halve the vanilla pod lengthways, scrape out the seeds and toss with the rhubarb, sugar and cornflour into a bowl. Once combined, add the rhubarb to your prepared dish.

To make the crumble, cube the butter, then toss with the flour. Cut into the flour with a cutlery knife until the butter is in small pieces.

Use your fingertips to rub the butter into the flour until the mixture resembles breadcrumbs with a few larger pieces of butter. Stir in the sugar and 1 pinch of sea salt.

Tip the crumble mixture over the rhubarb without pressing down. Place on a baking tray to catch any drips, and bake for 35 to 40 minutes, or until golden and bubbling. Serve with hot vanilla custard or cold cream. It also keeps well until the following day

28. Rice and Chicken

Ingredients

- ½ cup cooked Quinoa
- Handful Kale
- 1 piece of chicken - leg, breast or thigh are OK
- ½ red Capsicum
- ½ red Onion
- Handful baby spinach
- Cherry tomatoes

Sauce

- 1 tsp Lemon juice
- 1 tsp Olive oil
- 1 tsp Tahini
- 1 tablespoon water

Instructions

1. Cook to quinoa according to the instructions on the package.

Sprinkle a dash of lemon juice and olive oil and a pinch of salt over the chicken.

Slice the onion, capsicum and spread on a lined baking tray alongside the chicken. Roast for 20 minutes.

Keep checking the vegetables, you may need to take them out first if they are ready before the chicken.

While that is roasting, steam the kale until bright green. This will only take a few minutes.

When all is cooked, place all the ingredients in a bowl. To make the sauce, combine all ingredients.

29. Delicious & Nutritious Crispy Salmon

Ingredients

- 2 bunches asparagus, trimmed, halved
- 3 zucchini, trimmed, peeled into ribbons
- 1/2 cup fresh mint leaves
- 4 salmon fillets
- 1 1/2 tbs tamari
- 1 1/2 tbs mirin
- 1 tsp finely grated fresh ginger
- 1/2 tsp sesame oil

Instructions

1. Steam the asparagus until just tender and drain. Pour cold, running water over. Place the asparagus, zucchini and mint in a large bowl and toss to combine. Divide your salad among 4 serving plates.

2. Place a non-stick fry pan over medium heat and sprinkle with a little olive oil. Cook salmon with the skin side down for 2-3 minutes or until crisp. Turn over and cook for another 2-3 minutes or until cooked to your liking.

3. To make the dressing, combine the liquid ingredients in a small bowl.

4. Place the cooked salmon over the salad and drizzle with the dressing.

5. Enjoy!

30. Bread and Butter pudding

Ingredients

- 2 cups cream
- 1 1/2 cups milk
- 1/4 cup honey
- 4 eggs
- 8 slices spelt or wholemeal bread
- 2 medium bananas
- Greek yoghurt to serve
- 1 cinnamon stick
- 1 vanilla bean or 2 tsp vanilla essence
- 1 tbs brown sugar

Instructions

1.
    Preheat the oven to 180 degrees Celsius and lightly grease a casserole dish.

    In a medium saucepan combine the cream, milk, honey and cinnamon. Split the vanilla bean in hlf and scoop out the seeds with the back of a teaspoon. Stir over medium heat for 5-7 minutes until mixture is hot. Pour into a jug and let cool.

In a large bowl, whisk the eggs until light and frothy and then gradually whisk in the warm milk mixture.

Layer the bread slices and bananas alternately in the dish, slightly overlapping. Slowly pour the liquid mixture over the bread and banana until covered and sprinkle with sugar. Place in a larger baking dish and add just enough boiled water to come halfway up the sides of the dish.

Bake for 40-45 minutes or until pudding is set.

SNACKS

31. Lemon and Blueberry Muffin

Ingredients

- 2 cups rice flour
- 3 teaspoons baking powder
- 1 tsp vanilla
- 1/2 cup caster sugar
- 125 g butter melted and slightly cooled
- 1/4 cup milk
- 2 certified free range eggs
- 1 mashed banana
- 125g frozen blueberries
- zest of 1 lemon

Instructions

Preheat the oven to 180 degress C and line a 12 cup muffin pan. Sift the flour into a large bowl and stir in the sugar. In a separate large bowl, whisk together the butter, milk, eggs, banana, bleberries, lemon zest and vanilla. Make a well in the centre of the dry ingredients and add the liquid ingredients all at once. Stir in until just combined, making sure not to over mix.

Spoon into the pre prepared muffin cases and bake for 15-20 minutes until just golden brown. Cool in pan for a few minutes and then transfer to a wire rack.

32. Lemon cookie

Ingredients

- 125 g butter softened
- 100 g raw caster sugar
- 1 free-range egg
- 200 g gluten free flour
- 2 lemon zest
- ¼ teaspoon baking powder
- 1 pinch sea salt
- gluten free flour for dusting
- 3 tablespoons demerara sugar

Instructions

Preheat your oven to 180°C. Beat the butter and sugar in a bowl with an electric mixer until soft and creamy, then beat in the egg until the mixture is light and fluffy. Add the flour, lemon zest, baking powder and salt and mix slightly just until you have a ball of dough. Cover and place in the fridge for 2 hours, or until firm.

Roll out the dough on a floured surface until ½ cm thick. Cut out shapes and place on a grease proofed tray. Sprinkle with demerara sugar and bake for 10 to 12 minutes until the edges are light brown. Transfer to a wire rack to cool.

33. Vegetarian sausage rolls

Ingredients

- 2 teaspoons olive oil
- 4 green shallots, trimmed, thinly sliced
- 2 garlic cloves, crushed
- 350g pkt frozen chopped spinach, thawed or chopped fresh spinach leaves
- 350g fresh ricotta, crumbled
- 1/2 cup finely grated parmesan
- 1 egg, lightly whisked, plus 1, extra, whisked
- 2 tablespoons chopped fresh dill (optional)
- 1 finely grated lemon rind
- Good pinch of ground nutmeg
- 2 sheets frozen puff pastry, just thawed
- Tomato sauce, to serve

Instructions

Preheat oven to 200C/180C fan forced. Line 2 baking trays with baking paper.

Pour the oil into a heated, small frying pan over medium heat and sauté the shallots and garlic for about 2 minutes or until softened. Transfer to a large mixing bowl.

Using your hands, squeeze as much water as you can out of the spinach. Place the spinach in a large bowl and add the ricotta, parmesan, egg, dill (if using), lemon rind and nutmeg. Season well. Use your hands to mix until evenly combined.

Cut each sheet of pastry in half. Place one quarter of the spinach mixture in a log shape along one long edge. Brush the other side edge with extra egg. Close each end. Cut each roll into 3 pieces and place seam-side down on the prepared trays. Repeat with the remaining spinach mixture and pastry.

Use a sharp knife to cut the rolls crossways at 0.5cm intervals. Brush pastry with extra egg and bake for 25 minutes or until golden brown.

Serve with tomato sauce and salad.

Delicious Pancake

34. Pancake Mix

Ingredients

- 1 large free-range egg
- 1 cup of self-raising flour (to add a bit more health, substitute the self raising flour with oat, buckwheat or spealt
- flour mixed with 2 teaspoons of baking powder)
- 1 cup of milk
- sea salt

Toppings

- 200 g blueberries
- olive oil
- 4 tablespoons natural yoghurt

Instructions

1. Crack the egg into a large mixing bowl and add the flour, milk and a pinch of the salt. Whisk everything together until there are no lumps and you have a lovely, smooth batter.

2. If using the blueberries, fold those in gently.

3. Add about ½ teaspoon of oil into a warm frying pan on medium heat.

4. Add about 1 ladle of batter into the pan and spread out lightly.

5. Cook the pancakes for 1 to 2 minutes, or until little bubbles appear on the surface and the bases are golden, then use a fish slice to carefully flip them over.

6. When the pancakes are golden on both sides, use a fish slice to transfer the pancakes to a plate.

7. Continue with these steps until there is no batter left in the bowl.

8. Serve the pancakes straight away, topped with a dollop of natural yoghurt, and some extra berries, if you like.

35. Gluten Free Chocolate Chip Cookies

Ingredients

- 2 cups organic rolled oats
- 50 g flaked or desiccated coconut
- 60 g melted butter
- 60 g raw honey, organic maple syrup or rice syrup
- 1 organic egg
- 100 g block good quality 70% dark chocolate or dark chocolate chips

Instructions

1. Preheat your oven to 150 C.

2. Combine oats, coconut, melted butter, honey (or whichever sweetener you are using) and egg into a mixing bowl.

3. Mix through with your hands for a few minutes, until the cookie starts to come together.

4. If using a chocolate block, break into small pieces.

5. Add chocolate to the oats and mix through.

6. Using a teaspoon, form into 12 cookies.

7. Place onto a lined baking tray and flatten slightly with the back of a fork.

8. Bake for about 20 minutes or until golden.

9. Remove from the oven and cool completely. Enjoy.

36. Healthy Carrot cake

Ingredients

- 500 grated carrots
- 3 organic eggs
- 2 teaspoons vanilla extract or paste
- 2 teaspoons cinnamon
- ½ teaspoon nutmeg
- 350g almond meal
- 60 ml macadamia nut oil or olive oil
- ½ cup organic maple syrup or 1/4 cup raw organic honey
- 1 cup fresh blueberries or raisins
- 2 teaspoons gluten free baking powder
- Greek style yoghurt to serve

Ricotta Icing

- 1 ½ cups firm ricotta
- 2 teaspoons vanilla extract
- 1 tablespoon raw honey

Place the ricotta, vanilla and honey in a food processor for 30 seconds or until smooth. Spread evenly over the cake.

Instructions

1. Preheat your oven to 160 C / 320 F.

    Combine the carrots, eggs, vanilla, cinnamon, nutmeg, almond meal, oil, honey, raisins and baking powder.

    Mix well until combined.

    Pour into a prepared 20 cm baking tin.

    Bake for 1 – 1 ½ hours or until cooked through.

    Remove from the oven and cool completely in the tin. Once it is cool, turn out.

    Serve alone or topped with Greek style yoghurt or vanilla frosting.
    Keeps in the fridge for up to 5 days. You can also slice into single portions and freeze!

37. Awesome Blueberry Pancakes

Ingredients

- 1 large free-range egg
- 1 cup of self-raising flour
- 1 cup of milk
- 200 g blueberries
- olive oil
- 4 tablespoons natural yoghurt

Instructions

2. Crack the egg into a large mixing bowl, add the flour, milk and a tiny pinch of sea salt.

3. Whisk everything together until you have a lovely smooth batter, then fold through the blueberries.

4. Heat ½ a tablespoon of olive oil in a large non-stick frying pan over a medium heat, carefully tilting the pan to spread the oil out evenly.

5. Add a few ladles of batter to the pan, leaving space between each one so they have room to spread out slightly – each ladleful will make one pancake, and you'll need to work in batches.

6. Cook for 1 to 2 minutes, or until little bubbles appear on the surface and the bases are golden, then carefully flip them over.

7. When the pancakes are golden on both sides, remove to a plate.

8. Repeat with the remaining batter, adding a little more oil to the pan between batches, if needed.

9. Serve the pancakes while they're still hot, with a dollop of yoghurt and some extra fresh berries, if you like.

38. Zucchini slice

Ingredients

- 5 eggs
- pepper
- 1 large zucchini, grated
- 400 g carrot, sweet potato or pumpkin, peeled and grated
- 1 1/2 cups canned corn kernels or frozen peas, drained
- 1 medium brown onion, peeled and diced
- 2 tsp dried mixed herbs
- 3/4 cup wholemeal self-raising flour
- 1 cup cheddar cheese, grated
- olive oil
- 3 large tomatoes, sliced, optional
- green side salad, to serve

Instructions

1. Preheat oven to 200°C (180°C fan forced).

2. Whisk eggs in a medium jug, season with black pepper and set aside.

3. In a large bowl combine remaining ingredients except tomato. Add eggs and stir mixture until well combined.

4. Spray a large baking dish with oil. Pour in zucchini mix and flatten with a spoon. Cover with tomato slices arranged in a single layer.

5. Bake for 40-45 minutes or until firm and golden brown.

6. Rest in the pan for 10 minutes before dividing into 6 pieces and cutting into slices. Serve with a green side salad.

39. Apple Pie

Ingredients

- 140 g unsalted butter, (cold)
- 275 g plain flour, plus extra for dusting
- 1 lemon
- 1 large free-range egg yolk

Filling

- 9 apples
- 5 medjool dates pitted
- 4 tablespoons soft light muscovado sugar
- ¼ teaspoon ground cinnamon
- 1 pinch of ground cloves

Glaze

- 1 large free-range egg
- 1 teaspoon milk
- 1 tablespoon demerara sugar, plus extra for sprinkling

Instructions

1. Dice the butter and tip into the bowl of a food processor with the flour and ¼ of a teaspoon of sea

salt, then pulse until the mixture resembles coarse breadcrumbs. Finely grate the lemon zest and reserve for later, then squeeze in 1 tablespoon of lemon juice, add the egg yolk and 2 tablespoons of cold water, and pulse to combine. If the mixture is still looking a little dry, continue adding small amounts of water and pulsing until the dough comes together.

2. Divide the dough in two, shape into equal-sized discs, wrap in clingfilm and place in the fridge for 1 hour to firm up.

3. Peel and core the apples, cut into 1cm wedges and place in a saucepan. Sprinkle over the reserved lemon zest and squeeze in the remaining juice. Finely chop the dates, removing any pits, then stir in with the sugar and spices. Gently simmer over a medium-low heat for 6 to 8 minutes, or until the apples are almost tender. Set aside to cool.

4. Preheat the oven to 200°C. On a flour-dusted surface, roll out one pastry disc to 5mm thick and use it to line a deep 20cm pie dish, pushing the pastry into the edges. Trim the edges, leaving a 2.5cm overhang

around the dish. Spoon in the cooled pie filling, packing it tightly.

5. Roll out the second pastry disc to 5mm thick, moisten the edges with water and place over the pie, pressing the edges to seal. Fold in the overhang and crimp with your fingers.

6. Beat all the ingredients for the glaze in a small bowl, then brush all over the pie. If you have any off-cuts of pastry, you could make extra decorations for the top, sealing with extra glaze. Using a sharp knife, make incisions into the pie top to allow steam to escape during baking. Sprinkle with extra demerara sugar.

7. Bake the pie for 35 to 40 minutes, or until the pastry is golden and firm. Delicious served warm, with pouring cream or lashings of fresh custard.

40. Roasted Pumpkin Pikelets

Ingredients

- 2 heaped cups of Butternut pumpkin
- 2-3 Garlic cloves
- 1/3 of a cup of Spring Onion
- 1/2 a cup of gluten free flour such as Buckwheat or Coconut flour
- 1 teaspoon of gluten free Baking powder
- Splash of plant based milk such as Almond or Coconut Milk
- 2 free range Eggs
- 1-2 tablespoons of Coconut or Olive oil plus extra for frying
- ½ a teaspoon of Himalayan Crystal Salt
- ¼ of a teaspoon of freshly ground black pepper
- ¼ of a teaspoon of Smoky Paprika

Instructions

1. Cut the pumpkin into small cubes leaving the skin on.

2. Add the pumpkin, garlic, salt, pepper, paprika and melted coconut oil into a bowl and mix to coat the

pumpkin in the oil and seasoning before placing into a roasting pan.

3. Roast in a pre-heated oven at 180 degrees celcius until golden brown.

4. Allow to cool slightly before mashing roughly by hand, then add the flour,

5. baking powder, finely sliced spring onions and eggs. Mix together and add.

6. just enough milk to make a nice thick batter.

7. Heat oil in a frying pan and add approximately 2 tablespoons of batter per.

8. pikelet. Cook for 2 minutes each side until golden brown and bubbling.